JAMES JOYCE

Pomes Penyeach

Martino Publishing
Mansfield Centre, CT
2012

Martino Publishing
P.O. Box 373,
Mansfield Centre, CT 06250 USA

www.martinopublishing.com

ISBN   978-1-61427-318-9

Cover design by T. Matarazzo

Printed in the United States of America On 100% Acid-Free Paper

JAMES JOYCE

Pomes Penyeach

Shakespeare & Co.
Paris
1927

Pomes Penyeach
First published in 1927
by Shakespeare & Co., Paris

Contents

1   *Pomes Penyeach*

Tilly   page 13

Watching the Needleboats at San Sabba   14

A Flower given to my Daughter   15

She weeps over Rahoon   16

Tutto è Sciolto   17

On the Beach at Fontana   18

Simples   19

Flood   20

Nightpiece   21

Alone   22

A Memory of the Players in a Mirror at Midnight   23

Bahnhofstrasse   24

A Prayer   25

2   *Ecce Puer*   29

3   *The Holy Office*   33

4   *Gas from a Burner*   41

Publishers' Note

In order to make this volume more substantial and to show a wider range of James Joyce's verse, there have been added to *Pomes Penyeach* the following:

(i) *Ecce Puer*, originally published in *New Republic*, New York, November 30, 1932; reprinted in *The Criterion*, London, January 1933; included in *Collected Poems*, New York, 1936.

(ii) *The Holy Office*, originally published by James Joyce in 1904/1905.

(iii) *Gas from a Burner*, originally published by James Joyce in 1912.

The Holy Office and *Gas from a Burner* are included in *The Critical Writings of James Joyce* edited by Ellsworth Mason and Richard Ellmann (1959), to whom acknowledgements and thanks are due for permission to reprint here their notes to these poems.

Pomes Penyeach

Tilly

He travels after a winter sun,
Urging the cattle along a cold red road,
Calling to them, a voice they know,
He drives his beasts above Cabra.

The voice tells them home is warm.
They moo and make brute music with their hoofs.
He drives them with a flowering branch before him,
Smoke pluming their foreheads.

Boor, bond of the herd,
Tonight stretch full by the fire!
I bleed by the black stream
For my torn bough!

Dublin, 1904.

Watching the Needleboats
at San Sabba

I heard their young hearts crying
Loveward above the glancing oar
And heard the prairie grasses sighing:
No more, return no more!

O hearts, O sighing grasses,
Vainly your loveblown bannerets mourn!
No more will the wild wind that passes
Return, no more return.

Trieste, 1912.

A Flower given to my Daughter

Frail the white rose and frail are
Her hands that gave
Whose soul is sere and paler
Than time's wan wave.

Rosefrail and fair—yet frailest
A wonder wild
In gentle eyes thou veilest,
My blueveined child.

Trieste, 1913.

She weeps over Rahoon

Rain on Rahoon falls softly, softly falling,
Where my dark lover lies.
Sad is his voice that calls me, sadly calling,
At grey moonrise.

Love, hear thou
How soft, how sad his voice is ever calling,
Ever unanswered, and the dark rain falling,
Then as now.

Dark too our hearts, O love, shall lie and cold
As his sad heart has lain
Under the moongrey nettles, the black mould
And muttering rain.

Trieste, 1913.

Tutto è Sciolto

A birdless heaven, seadusk, one lone star
Piercing the west,
As thou, fond heart, love's time, so faint, so far,
Rememberest.

The clear young eyes' soft look, the candid brow,
The fragrant hair,
Falling as through the silence falleth now
Dusk of the air.

Why then, remembering those shy
Sweet lures, repine
When the dear love she yielded with a sigh
Was all but thine?

Trieste, 1914.

On the Beach at Fontana

Wind whines and whines the shingle,
The crazy pierstakes groan;
A senile sea numbers each single
Slimesilvered stone.

From whining wind and colder
Grey sea I wrap him warm
And touch his trembling fineboned shoulder
And boyish arm.

Around us fear, descending
Darkness of fear above
And in my heart how deep unending
Ache of love!

Trieste, 1914.

Simples

O bella bionda,
Sei come l'onda!

Of cool sweet dew and radiance mild
The moon a web of silence weaves
In the still garden where a child
Gathers the simple salad leaves.

A moondew stars her hanging hair
And moonlight kisses her young brow
And, gathering, she sings an air:
Fair as the wave is, fair, art thou!

Be mine, I pray, a waxen ear
To shield me from her childish croon
And mine a shielded heart for her
Who gathers simples of the moon.

Trieste, 1915.

Flood

Goldbrown upon the sated flood
The rockvine clusters lift and sway;
Vast wings above the lambent waters brood
Of sullen day.

A waste of waters ruthlessly
Sways and uplifts its weedy mane
Where brooding day stares down upon the sea
In dull disdain.

Uplift and sway, O golden vine,
Your clustered fruits to love's full flood,
Lambent and vast and ruthless as is thine
Incertitude!

Trieste, 1915.

Nightpiece

Gaunt in gloom,
The pale stars their torches,
Enshrouded, wave.
Ghostfires from heaven's far verges faint illume,
Arches on soaring arches,
Night's sindark nave.

Seraphim,
The lost hosts awaken
To service till
In moonless gloom each lapses muted, dim,
Raised when she has and shaken
Her thurible.

And long and loud,
To night's nave upsoaring,
A starknell tolls
As the bleak incense surges, cloud on cloud,
Voidward from the adoring
Waste of souls.

Trieste, 1915.

Alone

The moon's greygolden meshes make
All night a veil,
The shorelamps in the sleeping lake
Laburnum tendrils trail.

The sly reeds whisper to the night
A name—her name—
And all my soul is a delight,
A swoon of shame.

Zurich, 1916.

A Memory of the Players in
a Mirror at Midnight

They mouth love's language. Gnash
The thirteen teeth
Your lean jaws grin with. Lash
Your itch and quailing, nude greed of the flesh.
Love's breath in you is stale, worded or sung,
As sour as cat's breath,
Harsh of tongue.

This grey that stares
Lies not, stark skin and bone.
Leave greasy lips their kissing. None
Will choose her what you see to mouth upon.
Dire hunger holds his hour.
Pluck forth your heart, saltblood, a fruit of tears.
Pluck and devour!

Zurich, 1917.

Bahnhofstrasse

The eyes that mock me sign the way
Whereto I pass at eve of day,

Grey way whose violet signals are
The trysting and the twining star.

Ah star of evil! star of pain!
Highhearted youth comes not again

Nor old hearts' wisdom yet to know
The signs that mock me as I go.

Zurich, 1918.

A Prayer

Again!
Come, give, yield all your strength to me!
From far a low word breathes on the breaking brain
Its cruel calm, submission's misery,
Gentling her awe as to a soul predestined.
Cease, silent love! My doom!

Blind me with your dark nearness, O have mercy,
     beloved enemy of my will!
I dare not withstand the cold touch that I dread.
Draw from me still
My slow life! Bend deeper on me, threatening head,
Proud by my downfall, remembering, pitying
Him who is, him who was!

Again!
Together, folded by the night, they lay on earth. I hear
From far her low word breathe on my breaking brain.
Come ! I yield. Bend deeper upon me! I am here.
Subduer, do not leave me! Only joy, only anguish,
Take me, save me, soothe me, O spare me!

Paris, 1924.

Ecce Puer

Ecce Puer

Of the dark past
A child is born;
With joy and grief
My heart is torn.

Calm in his cradle
The living lies.
May love and mercy
Unclose his eyes!

Young life is breathed
On the glass;
The world that was not
Comes to pass.

A child is sleeping:
An old man gone.
O, father forsaken,
Forgive your son!

The Holy Office

The Holy Office[1]

Joyce composed this satirical broadside about two months before he left Dublin in 1904. He had it printed but could not afford to pay for it, so the following year, in Pola, he had it printed again and sent the sheets to his brother Stanislaus for distribution to the butts of his satire in Dublin.

In the poem he lumps together Yeats and Russell and their followers, accusing them all of hypocrisy and self-deception. One would hardly suspect from their writings that they had bodies at all; their spirituality has its analogue in female prudery. Joyce, who had always prided himself on his candour and honesty, and was now demonstrating these qualities in Stephen Hero *and the first stories of* Dubliners, *yokes Aristotle to Christian ritual to claim that his own office is Katharsis, the revelation of what the mummers hide. Then, elevating his metaphor, he condemns them from the mountain-top to which Ibsen and Nietzsche had helped to bring him.*

Myself unto myself will give
This name, Katharsis-Purgative.
I, who dishevelled ways forsook
To hold the poets' grammar-book,[2]

---

[1] The title refers ironically to (1) the office of confession, and (2) the department of the church that launched the Inquisition, and that today exercises the function of censorship. There are also overtones of 'the holy office an ostler does for the stallion', *Ulysses,* p. 200 (191).

[2] Joyce collected the solecisms in the works of his eminent contemporaries.

Bringing to tavern and to brothel
The mind of witty Aristotle,
Lest bards in the attempt should err
Must here be my interpreter:
Wherefore receive now from my lip
Peripatetic scholarship.
To enter heaven, travel hell,
Be piteous or terrible,
One positively needs the ease
Of plenary indulgences.
For every true-born mysticist
A Dante is, unprejudiced,[1]
Who safe at ingle-nook, by proxy,
Hazards extremes of heterodoxy,
Like him who finds a joy at table,
Pondering the uncomfortable.
Ruling one's life by commonsense
How can one fail to be intense?
But I must not accounted be
One of that mumming company[2]—

[1] Repeated from Joyce's essay on Ibsen's *Catalina.*
[2]   *Know that I would accounted be*
         True brother of a company
         That sang, to sweeten Ireland's wrong . . .
         Yeats, 'Address to Ireland in the Coming Times'.

With him[1] who hies him to appease

His giddy dames'[2] frivolities

While they console him when he whinges

With gold-embroidered Celtic fringes[3]—

Or him who sober all the day

Mixes a naggin in his play[4]—

Or him whose conduct 'seems to own'

His preference for a man of 'tone'[5]—

Or him who plays the ragged patch

To millionaires in Hazelhatch

But weeping after holy fast

Confesses all his pagan past[6]—

Or him who will his hat unfix

Neither to malt nor crucifix

But show to all that poor-dressed be

The 'mumming company' is used as a general derogatory label, but has also a specific reference to the Abbey Theatre, which received its patent in August, 1904. Sponsored financially by Annie E. Horniman, headed by Lady Augusta Gregory, and artistically dominated by Yeats, it had grown out of the earlier Irish National Theatre, and almost all the young Irish writers except Joyce had some share in one group or the other.

[1] Yeats.

[2] Lady Gregory and Miss Horniman, and perhaps Maud Gonne MacBride.

[3] An allusion to the gilt decorations on the books that Yeats published in the 1890's.

[4] John Synge.   [5] Oliver Gogarty.   [6] Padraic Colum.

His high Castilian courtesy[1]—
Or him who loves his Master dear[2]—
Or him who drinks his pint in fear[3]—
Or him who once when snug abed
Saw Jesus Christ without his head
And tried so hard to win for us
The long-lost works of Eschylus.[4]
But all these men of whom I speak
Make me the sewer of their clique.
That they may dream their dreamy dreams
I carry off their filthy streams
For I can do those things for them
Through which I lost my diadem,
Those things for which Grandmother Church
Left me severely in the lurch.
Thus I relieve their timid arses,
Perform my office of Katharsis.
My scarlet leaves them white as wool.[5]

[1] W. K. Magee ('John Eglinton').
[2] George Roberts, a devoted follower of George Russell, who addressed Russell in this way in a poem.
[3] James S. Starkey ('Seumas O'Sullivan').
[4] George Russell.
[5] 'Though your sins be as scarlet, they shall be as white as snow.' Isaiah 1:18.

Through me they purge a bellyful.
To sister mummers one and all
I act as vicar-general,[1]
And for each maiden, shy and nervous,
I do a similar kind service.
For I detect without surprise
That shadowy beauty in her eyes,
The 'dare not' of sweet maidenhood
That answers my corruptive 'would'.[2]
Whenever publicly we meet
She never seems to think of it;
At night when close in bed she lies
And feels my hand between her thighs
My little love in light attire
Knows the soft flame that is desire.
But Mammon places under ban
The uses of Leviathan[3]
And that high spirit ever wars
On Mammon's countless servitors,

[1] A bishop's assistant, who handles operational details of the diocese.

[2] *Letting 'I dare not' wait upon 'I would',*
Like the poor cat i' the adage.
                    Macbeth, I, vii, 44-5.

[3] The heroic, individualistic Satan; here Joyce.

37

Nor can they ever be exempt
From his taxation of contempt.
So distantly I turn to view
The shamblings of that motley crew,
Those souls that hate the strength that mine has
Steeled in the school of old Aquinas.
Where they have crouched and crawled and prayed
I stand the self-doomed, unafraid,
Unfellowed, friendless and alone,
Indifferent as the herring-bone,
Firm as the mountain-ridges where
I flash my antlers on the air.[1]
Let them continue as is meet
To adequate the balance-sheet.
Though they may labour to the grave
My spirit shall they never have
 Nor make my soul with theirs as one
Till the Mahamanvantara[2] be done:
And though they spurn me from their door
My soul shall spurn them evermore.

[1] 'There was his ground and he flung them disdain from flash-ing antlers.' *Stephen Hero*, p. 35 (27).
[2] The Hindu great year.

Gas from a Burner

Gas from a Burner

In September 1909, Joyce, then on a visit to Dublin, signed a contract with the Dublin firm of Maunsel and Co. to publish Dubliners. *But George Roberts, the manager of the firm, began to find reasons first for delaying and then for censoring the manuscript. Negotiations dragged along for three years, until finally Joyce returned to Dublin in July 1912, and brought the matter to a head. Both Joyce and Roberts consulted solicitors; Roberts was advised that the use of actual names for public houses and the like was libellous, and began to demand so many changes that there was no possibility of agreement. At length he decided to accept Joyce's offer to purchase the sheets for the book, which John Falconer, a Dublin printer, had finished. But Falconer, hearing of the dispute, decided he wanted nothing to do with so unpleasant a book, and guillotined the sheets. Joyce left Dublin full of bitterness, which he vented by writing this broadside on the back of his contract with Maunsel and Co. for the publication of* Dubliners, *while he was on the train between Flushing and Salzburg.*

Ladies and gents, you are here assembled
To hear why earth and heaven trembled
Because of the black and sinister arts
Of an Irish writer in foreign parts.
He sent me a book ten years ago.[1]
I read it a hundred times or so,
Backwards and forwards, down and up,

[1] George Roberts is the speaker.

Through both ends of a telescope.
I printed it all to the very last word
But by the mercy of the Lord
The darkness of my mind was rent
And I saw the writer's foul intent.
But I owe a duty to Ireland:
I hold her honour in my hand,
This lovely land that always sent
Her writers and artists to banishment
And in a spirit of Irish fun
Betrayed her own leaders, one by one.
'Twas Irish humour, wet and dry,
Flung quicklime into Parnell's eye;[1]
'Tis Irish brains that save from doom
The leaky barge of the Bishop of Rome
For everyone knows the Pope can't belch
Without the consent of Billy Walsh.[2]
O Ireland my first and only love
Where Christ and Caesar are hand and glove!
O lovely land where the shamrock grows!

[1] This incident, which Joyce also mentions in 'The Shade of
Parnell' (p. 227 above) occurred at Castlecomer in the summer
of 1891, according to Parnell's biographer and friend, R. Barry
O'Brien.
[2] His Grace the Most Reverend William J. Walsh, D.D.,
Archbishop of Dublin.

(Allow me, ladies, to blow my nose)
To show you for strictures I don't care a button
I printed the poems of Mountainy Mutton[1]
And a play he wrote (you've read it I'm sure)
Where they talk of 'bastard', 'bugger' and 'whore'[2]
And a play on the Word and Holy Paul
And some woman's legs that I can't recall
Written by Moore, a genuine gent
That lives on his property's ten per cent:[3]
I printed mystical books in dozens:
I printed the table-book of Cousins[4]

[1] Joseph Campbell, author of *The Mountainy Singer*, published by Maunsel in 1909.

[2] Campbell's *Judgment: a Play in Two Acts*, published by Maunsel in 1912, contains on p. 25 the words 'bastard' and 'whore'.

[3] *The Apostle*, published by Maunsel in 1911. Moore's play, in which Christ (the Word) and Paul meet after Christ's death, includes a dialogue between Christ and Mary in which Mary laments her lost beauty. In a long preface Moore surveys the Bible for evidence of sensuality and remarks (p. 9) 'In Samuel we read how David was captured by the sweetness of Bathsheba's legs while bathing . . .', and (p. 26) 'It may be doubted whether Paul always succeeded in subduing these infirmities of the flesh, but we would not love him less, even if we knew that he had loved St. Eunice not wisely but too well.'

[4] James Cousins, a Dublin Theosophist and poet. The 'table-book' is probably his *Etain the Beloved and Other Poems*, published by Maunsel in 1912.

Though (asking your pardon) as for the verse
'Twould give you a heartburn on your arse:[1]
I printed folklore from North and South
By Gregory of the Golden Mouth:[2]
I printed poets, sad, silly and solemn:
I printed Patrick What-do-you-Colm:[3]
I printed the great John Milicent Synge
Who soars above on an angel's wing
In the playboy shift[4] that he pinched as swag
From Maunsel's manager's travelling-bag.[5]
But I draw the line at that bloody fellow,
That was over here dressed in Austrian yellow,
Spouting Italian by the hour
To O'Leary Curtis[6] and John Wyse Power[7]
And writing of Dublin, dirty and dear,

[1] An expression of Joyce's father; see *Ulysses*, p. 122 (115).
[2] Maunsel published Lady Gregory's *Kiltartan History Book* in 1909 and *The Kiltartan Wonder Book* in 1910.
[3] Padraic Colum.
[4] The word 'shift', spoken by a character in Synge's *Playboy of the Western World* caused a riot at the Abbey Theatre in 1907; Maunsel published the play in the same year.
[5] Roberts was a traveller in ladies' underwear.
[6] A Dublin journalist.
[7] An official in the Royal Irish Constabulary in Dublin Castle, and a man of considerable cultivation. He figures largely in *Ulysses* in the characters of Jack Power and John Wyse Nolan.

In a manner no blackamoor printer could bear.
Shite and onions![1] Do you think I'll print
The name of the Wellington Monument,
Sydney Parade and Sandymount tram,
Downes's cakeshop and Williams's jam?
I'm damned if I do—I'm damned to blazes!
Talk about *Irish Names of Places!*[2]
It's a wonder to me, upon my soul,
He forgot to mention Curly's Hole.[3]
No, ladies, my press shall have no share in
So gross a libel on Stepmother Erin.[4]
I pity the poor—that's why I took
A red-headed Scotchman[5] to keep my book.
Poor sister Scotland! Her doom is fell;
She cannot find any more Stuarts to sell.
My conscience is fine as Chinese silk:
My heart is as soft as buttermilk.

[1] An expression of Joyce's father; see *Ulysses*, p. 125 (117).
[2] *The Origin and History of Irish Names of Places*, by Patrick Weston Joyce, no relation to James.
[3] A bathing pool at Dollymount, Clontarf.
[4] As Dr. Oliver Gogarty remarks, in *Mourning Becomes Mrs. Spendlove* (N.Y., 1948) p. 61, Roberts was an Ulster Scot, so Erin is only his stepmother.
[5] Roberts himself.

Colm can tell you I made a rebate
Of one hundred pounds on the estimate
I gave him for his Irish Review.[1]
I love my country—by herrings I do!
I wish you could see what tears I weep
When I think of the emigrant train and ship.
That's why I publish far and wide
My quite illegible railway guide.
In the porch of my printing institute
The poor and deserving prostitute
Plays every night at catch-as-catch-can
With her tight-breeched British artilleryman
And the foreigner learns the gift of the gab
From the drunken draggletail Dublin drab.
Who was it said: Resist not evil?[2]
I'll burn that book, so help me devil.
I'll sing a psalm as I watch it burn
  And the ashes I'll keep in a one-handled urn.
I'll penance do with farts and groans
Kneeling upon my marrowbones.
This very next lent I will unbare

[1] The *Irish Review* was edited by Colum from March 1912–July 1913.
[2] Christ, in the Sermon on the Mount.

My penitent buttocks to the air
And sobbing beside my printing press
My awful sin I will confess.
My Irish foreman from Bannockburn[1]
Shall dip his right hand in the urn
And sign crisscross with reverent thumb
Memento homo[2] upon my bum.

[1] In Scotland.
[2] 'Memento, homo, quia pulvis es', the words of the priest on Ash Wednesday as he marks the cross of ashes on the communicant's forehead.

CPSIA information can be obtained
at www.ICGtesting.com
Printed in the USA
BVHW03s2358240718
522561BV00001B/12/P